How to Rap:

Elementary Teachings of Hip-Hop

By Hitachi Choparazzi

How to Rap: Elementary Teachings of Hip-Hop

©Copyright 2020

All Rights Reserved

By Hitachi Choparazzi

Chop-A-Style Publishing LLC

LCCN: 2022902466

ISBN: 979-8-9857661-5-8

Dedication

I dedicate this book to my sons and all the youth for generations to come.

I asked one of my sons if he can rap since he loves hip-hop and is a huge fan. He said he didn't know how to.

My other son has more of a conscious rapper style, like Common, but didn't know. He also wrote a nice rhyme, but he was freestyling. Discovery is pivotal.

So I decided to write a how to rap book, to educate not just my sons, but all the youth. Girls, too. There are some dope artists and we need way more in the industry. All creeds, genders, races, etc. It's all welcome to educate themselves on hip-hop.

Education is key, and I want to give the youth an outline and structure to create their own space according to the hip-hop culture.

I love y'all...the youth is the truth. Pursue your endeavors and listen to the vibrations of your heart.

ATTN:

This *How to Rap* book is simply a guide to show you how to start and structure. This book is not entitling you or promising you a record deal or to go platinum plus. Nor to make you turn automatic superstar.

This book is to give you direction and show you how to develop original content as an outline.

This book is meant to inspire, innovate, motivate and educate you only.

Acknowledgements

First and foremost, all due praise to the Creator for blessing me with life and spirit to have the ability to write along with all my gifts to the world.

All my Luv1s, sons Kolany Jr., Pierre Kydale, Kylan, and beautiful intelligent daughter China; Dad loves y'all uncontrollably. My G-Ma Lawson, the Queen of the Tribe, Blessns.

My Luv1s that passed away. Rest in Harmony, G-Pa Lawson, Unc Dale, Lil Bro Peppy (Pierre) and all my Day1s. I do this for y'all. The latest Disean P. Russell. RIP.

Chop-A-Style Publishing LLC, Billion Dollar Blueprint movement and the youth movement representing education, elevation, and innovation. All my NYC, Midwest & Down South family. All my friends, fans, associates city-to-city. Thanks for believing me and being my motivation and inspiration. Peace and Blessns.

Contents

Introduction

Hip-hop is 45 years old as of 2018. Birthplace Bronx, NY. It is now international and constantly evolving with different elements.

Hip-hop is perpetual. Don't be afraid to add different elements to it or step out the box.

Rap is rhythm. Deliver your rhythm and vibes. Rap has always been the gateway for other opportunities and a platform to stand on once you establish yourself as a household name.

From original roots of break-dancing, Bboxing, battle rapping, fashion, and lyrical play is all hip-hop.

Rap is a verbal medium. Your words are used to tell the story or paint a picture or how to move your feet and do a type of dance.

An M.C. is abbreviated for Master of Ceremonies, which what a rapper is. And a D.J. is a Disc Jockey, who plays, mixes, and even produces music, too.

I am a musicologist, which is the study of music as a field of knowledge or research.

The jungle, a cave, the desert, and the woodlands all have a certain sound to them. If you can, tune in and listen to their melody. After you tune out everything else. And you can use this same method to develop your sound, your ear, your melody inside of you. Bring that unique sound to the world to hear and feel your vibration. They will move in harmony with you, guaranteed.

The questions you ask yourself:

Who am I?

What am I?

What's my message?

What's my story?

My movement, goal, challenge?

How can I manifest and master it?

I don't believe in no such thing as a bad artist. Everyone is a unique artist and have individuality. I respect all people creative space and works of art.

Now, there is a such thing as bad music because of lack of knowledge and education. Whether it's from delivery, off-key, non-rhythmic, or a flat-out mediocre hook and beat. Unless you're simply not talented in the rap or hip-hop field as a whole, then it's not your career path.

As long as you stay on tempo with your melody and rhythm of the beat and master your sound, you will have the art form down. Stage presence, catching and riding the beat takes practice, but you have to have drive and really work at perfecting your newfound craft to be great. Unless you just doing it as a hobby. You'll prosper times 10 at developing, and will discover new ways as more tunes come to your head and heart to breathe life into them.

Don't sound like everyone else on the radio or favorite rapper you grew up listening to.

Create and build you, develop your own unique sound. Then let the world discover you!

Trust me, they love new. The newest car, food, and song. You can be the NBT (Next Big Thing).

- Chapter 1 -

"A Bar" (Bars)

This chapter is the beginning step and the format that artists use to create music and lyrics. This is the platform that your verbal rap medium is projected.

A bar in musical terms is a vertical line across 3 musical staff. A musical staff is 5 horizontal lines on which music is written. And a line is a horizontal row of written verse.

Rap is to talk freely and frankly, a rhythmic chanting of rhymed couplets to a musical accompaniment. So to create a bar, it has to rhyme, which is why you need 2 lines to complete your first bar.

For example:

Line 1 She say she loves me...

Line 2 I'm thinking money...

Now the word "me" at the end of line 1, is the start of a bar. It's the first half. You have to do a brief pause so your audience recognizes that you're going to spit something that rhymes with "me." So on line 2 to complete your first bar, end with the word "money."

Your word play doesn't have to be spelled the same. Just as long as you get them to sound the same in a rhythmic still, you can play with and adjust them.

However, you can follow up after first bar is complete with 2 lines; with one-line bars, or you can stick with 2 lines per bar.

For example:

Line 1   She say she loves me...

Line 2   I'm thinking money...

Line 3   No time for honey...

Line 4   Just sold out overseas...

In line 3, the last word "honey," is a one-line bar and the same with line 4, the end word "seas." So far that is a total of 3 bars on 4 lines.

Now to give you inner urban culture words used by hip-hop communities and industry. When they say the "bar" or "bars," it's used in a form of lyrical word play of urban subculture meaning delivery, so you have to really bring it on each bar like a punchline. Make every one felt. If someone says, "Hey, you got bars," or "Dope bars," take it as a compliment.

Lyrical bars are tied to artists like Nas. Not all rappers have dope bars. Some of their bars are so predictable that people say them before the artist. Or simply yawn, which some associate to be ABC Cat-in-the-Hat rap.

Remember M.C. is to master, so this is key to first get down pat. The cool thing about hip-hop is you create your own sound and plenty of creative space. You have to master this format to become a pro.

Some rappers like Jay-Z and Lil Wayne have been known and notorious for freestyling off the top of their head all their bars, which is a true God-given talent not everyone has, but you can work at it.

As a beginner, I personally wouldn't recommend it unless you are a natural. I think when you sit down and write bar-for-bar, you can have time to think and create more effective lyrics.

Verse freestyling recording your bars straight to a track. When you freestyle, it's usually impulse, and people usually say whatever is the first thing that comes to mind.

I'm not against it because I'm sure Jay-Z has a way he formulates his bars in his head and memorizes them all verbatim when on stage.

Work on your craft and you will find whatever you're comfortable with or comes more natural.

I like sitting down and handwriting each bar. However, you can simply use your electronic device. Talk-to-text or manually text/type the lyrics in bar-for-bar.

In writing bars, make sure it doesn't conflict and go against your theme or what type of rapper you are. Also what you're promoting or stand for. Basically don't go against the grain. Remember it's a verbal medium you are pushing, so sound is everything and the people are always listening.

Next step I'll show you an example on how to continue to build and count your bars from the previous 2 methods of producing your initial bar and bars with that format.

For example:

Line 1   She say she loves me...

Line 2   I'm thinking money...

Line 3   No time for honey...

Line 4   Just sold out overseas...

Line 5   Plus her friend ugly...

Line 6   Skirt out in Bugatti...

Line 7   She say I'm being funny...

Line 8   Sorry baby I'm no dummy...

Line 9   Skirt-skirt! Switch lanes...

Line 10   My subject I had to change...

Line 11   Bling-bling! In my pinky rang...

Line 12   So Icy like Gucci Mane...

Line 13   This history in the making...

Line 14   It all started out from rapping...

Line 15   Please pinch me, I'm dreaming...

Line 16   Like Jim Jones I'm balling...

Line 17   In the rap game I'm all in...

Line 18   A shooting star that's never falling...

You have to first catch the melody and the tempo set on the song. A trick to this method is drag out the last word on every bar until you catch the rhythm for delivery. There is a such thing called run-on bars, just like run-on sentences.

You do not want your bars being pro se speeches. Instead short, direct, to the point, and on key with delivery. This is the beauty of this art form because it's so versatile. This is your creative space to word play.

In the example above, I wrote 18 lines with a total of 15 bars, which is one shy of a 16.

On line 9, the last word "lanes" starts for a new bar, same way we did in line 1 and line 2. Now line 10 last word "change" completes one bar. So every time you change your last word at the end of a line, it starts and is the automatic setup for a new bar to follow.

On line 13, the last word "making" starts a new bar. Line 14 last word "rapping" completes another bar. Following line 15 "dreaming" the last word, which is only one line, but again another one-line bar. Same with line 16.

What helps me when I don't get something, I reread and study it until I grasp it. And that's what I recommend you do, until you can count the bars up correctly to know how many you are actually delivering.

To your surprise, you may be scratching your head how many artists don't know how to count their bars. Some songs are like 10 to 12 bars, not a full 16 bars. I have actually heard an artist spit 8, and obviously he wasn't in the industry too long.

So it is really important to educate yourself. A person can charge or pay upper ranges between $100 to $250k for a hot 16. What if they only give you 9 bars and you got the hottest single streaming in the nation? That's how a lot of people lose out or fail in this cutthroat industry. Knowledge is key.

This your first step to becoming an M.C. Remember your bars set the tone and speak volumes while gathering the attention of the masses. Also this is the start to developing your own sound. Don't be afraid to try other styles and effects.

- Chapter 2 -

"A 16" (Verse)

The art of storytelling starts here with the sweet science to your core rhyming melody. This is your canvas to paint your clear picture with your lyrics and sound.

A 16 is 16 bars total. Also known as an actual verse. It is usually 3 verses to complete a song.

Nowadays most artists only do 2 verses total or 1 verse with 1 or 2 featured artists. Sometimes 3 or 4 featured artists, which is more like a compilation than a collaboration.

Tupac Shakur specialized in writing a 16 with 3 verses in a lot of his music. He also didn't have a lot of featured artists on a lot of his albums.

So I would recommend you do at least 2 verses as standard nowadays all artists seem to adapt. Of course it's less creative work, but you can do 3 verses if you so please. Also, some artists don't like 5-minute songs as they did 20 years ago.

Now I am about to give you an example of a 16.

Example: A 16

Line 1   Everybody say they got bars

Line 2   But only spit about foreign cars

Line 3   And ballin like a all-star

Line 4   You better use ya OnStar

Line 5   Spit bars like a Mac II

Line 6   I'm bustin like a FN 5.7

Line 7   A handgun that shoot 223s

Line 8   Like Rambo I'm choppin down M.C.s

Line 9   Bars be so ill

Line 10   Putting cappers in a pickle like dill

Line 11   Even when I'm cold I don't chill

Line 12   You not signed still

Line 13   Boasting saying ya really-real

Line 14   With Lays you can't get a deal

Line 15   Them nursery rhymes nobody feel

Line 16   Mann...my bars vicious

Line 17   Do them dirty like dishes

Line 18   If they try to diss this

Line 19   Take em to class and dismiss

Line 20   #1 on ya girl playlist

I wrote a 16 on 20 lines. A total of 16 bars using 20 lines to do it. It can be up to 32 lines for a 16 if you do all line bars, which is rare but possible.

A lot of rappers are self-taught and don't take time out to read or write music. Not every rapper is going to be lyrical, so don't exhaust yourself competing early on. Just get your story and message out.

Another trick of the trade is if some of your line bars are longer than other short line bars, which it happens all in creative space, you simply speed up the words, meaning say the words faster to customize them to a tailor fit.

Also remember you can drag out or put emphasis on your last rhyming word on each bar, or shorter and longer pauses at the end of each bar. Practice out loud and in the mirror so you can hear and see yourself. Trust me, it helps.

You can also add an intro before your 16. Like say your name or an ad lib and signature sound. Some rappers can't stop saying their name, while others use sound effects or make shooting noises. Some may be silly or ludicrous, but again it's all creative art. And you're entitled to your own creative sound. This can be done at the beginning or end of your 16.

I'd highly recommend this method to new M.C.s to let the people know who you are and get familiar with your sound and voice. At least till your voice speaks volume to the fans.

Let this be your strong suit. Master this, your blueprint. You don't have to reinvent the wheel of rap, just invent your signature style.

The key is to do whatever you can manifest the best in an original sound and way. I want you to become the dopest version of yourself. Master your craft and self. Regardless of gender, race, age, or image. Be the best at you and eyes on the prize.

Don't be afraid to follow your dreams or scared to fail and trying something new. Nor to go out your comfort zone or stick to it.

And remember you can use old remedies with new tactics. This is part of innovation creating your canvas vibrant. And your lyrics are words to your song, verse, and hook that you use to project your inner energy out to the world in your rhythm to vibe to.

Now that you're getting a feel on how to produce and project on your verbal platform, you are on your way to becoming not just a dope M.C., but an educated and innovative one. Hip-hop is devotees of rap. Stylized rhythmic music to rap.

Your versification, which is the making of a verse to set your tune and have fun with it. You'll master versify.

- Chapter 3 -

"Hook" (Chorus)

A hook is a chorus, a part of song repeated. Hip-hop culture calls it a hook because its intention is to hook and catch you.

Now this is heart of your song and where your creative mindset have to kick in. Because even when people or your audience don't quite tune in well or catch all your lyrics verbatim, they will remember your hook, especially if it's catchy.

Some rappers have heavy accents, mumbles, or simply way too fast to keep up with. Others are simply inaudible but usually have a spot-on image or moves that move the crowd.

The hook's repeated effect gets people going and to sing along with you. It makes them familiar with the song or identify the song. And usually the artist names the song after or part of the hook.

Hooks are versatile, too. It's a few different methods you can use formulating your hook. They can be used at the beginning of the song, which is optional because some artists start off with straight bars and lyrics or simply talking.

Then they will come back with the hook after each verse. So after you spit your 16, then the hook follows consecutively.

Usually you hear the hook about 3 to 4 times in one song. However, again it is versatile and there is no set way or rule of thumb. And you can adjust and fine-tune to your speed. This is what I love about hip-hop, all the creative space for artists to propel their vibes and identity.

Some hooks are one word. It's optional.

Example:

Hook Hitachi-Hitachi-Hitachi!

Other hooks are sung by artist or feature artist and even sampled, while other hooks are concoctions with rapping and singing. Some are harmonized, a method and element Bone Thugs-N-Harmony brought to the table that Drake uses successfully.

While I even heard utter noises hook combos like the Ying-Yang Twins formulated.

There is no right or wrong way to do your hook, just make it count.

Now I will show you some examples on how to formulate your hooks since you have a nice feel for it already.

You want to start them just like your method for formulating your bars. It's all still hip-hop, so you want them to rhyme in sync. And remember, no long drag-on hooks. You don't want your audience to confuse your hook for lyrics. That isn't a good look and wouldn't last 10 seconds at the Apollo in Harlem.

And just like your verses and bars, you don't want to sound like every other hook on the radio unless, again, you're truly doing this as a hobby.

It's considered biting, and you don't want to bite off anybody's hook or style because it hinders the world from your own unique style. Blockages are never good because it could be blocking you from your blessing. You never know who is listening or watching. It could be ARs or executive producers that think your unique form is vibrant and dope from all your original works and want to help you bring that sound to the world using their multimillion-dollar platform already established.

Example: Hook

    Line 1 Like Jay-Z and Nip

    Line 2 Hitachii, got that Billion Dollar Blueprint

    Line 3 It's not a challenge, it's a movement

    Line 4 Education, Elevation, Innovation

    Line 5 They hating

Repeat lines 1 thru 3 once

Then spit lines 4 and 5 following the repeat. So you say the hook twice, then lines 4 and 5 after as second part or bottom half of the hook.

Then you follow it up with a sweet 16. This is another example of a hook.

You can even try a more settled approach with a 2-word hook, but repeated more times than a longer or mid-range hook. For example:

Example: 2-Word Hook

    Line 1 Hitachi-Choparazzi-Aye

Line 2 Hitachi-Choparazzi-Aye

Line 3 Hitachi-Choparazzi-Aye

Line 4 Hitachi-Hitachi-Hitachii!!

Repeat hook, then follow with verse

On this 2-word hook example, you say all 4 lines right after each other in sequence because the hook is short. Afterwards you repeat the hook again. Short hooks are usually more catchy because it's easier to remember and catch on to verse a few liens of different sentences, especially that sounds more like bars vs. a hook. Line 4 is what you call the sinker of the hook, which caps it off like a finale.

The next example is of a singing hook. Some artists can't sing but still sing their own hooks and use special effects like autotunes and other special features to enhance or alter your voice. It's so many just like filters to name. Some consider this cheating, but remember, no hating because anything goes, and it's still someone's respective work of art. And I know you will go a lot further as artist and people for respect artist special project usually they put their hearts, sweat, and tears into.

Example: Singing Hook

Line 1   Who loves you better than me, girl

Line 2   Who loves you better than me, girl *[emphasis on "girl"]*

Line 3   Who does you better than me, girl

Line 4   Who gets you anything in the world *[emphasis on "world"]*

Repeat singing hook, then follow with verse.

The singing hooks are catchy, too. However, you have to project your hook correct so the crowd catches your melody.

Lines 1 and 3 you sing normal with an even tempo. However, lines 2 and 4 you put emphasis on the last words and drag them out a little, either or same difference. Also, lines 2 and 4 are your hook and sinker lines. So do a great job at identifying which once you are in your creative process.

The examples above show you the basic ways of hooks and methods, but sky is the limit. Adjust and create the way you feel it comes to you. Just use this formula of doing a hook and not a verse for a hook or a run-on hook. And that's really the dos and don'ts.

Remember the hook sequence.

Example #1

1. Hook (Began)

2. Verse

3. Hook

4. Verse

5. Hook (End)

Example #2

1. Verse (Began)

2. Hook

3. Verse

4. Hook (End)

These are typical hooks format. Example 1, start off with a hook first, then a verse with another hook in the middle, followed by another verse and ending with a hook to cap song off.

Whereas in example 2, start off with a verse going straight into a 16, then a hook followed by a second verse and capping off with a hook at the end.

Okay, now are you ready for the flip side of this?

However, there is a such thing as a no-hook or chorus song. Yes, just straight bars. And an artist known for this and going outside the box is The Game.

The Game spit a 64-bar straight song, no hook. It was dope. Yes, a total of 4 verses. A 16, 4 times non-stop. A few other rappers have tried this type straight-bars, no-hook method. But you really need skills to spit high-impact bars straight thru non-stop.

While others do 2 hooks in one as one big hook. So develop your sound and grasp your melodies vibrating inside you and execute that same sound to the world.

You know that tune inside your head, but when it comes out, it don't sound the same. You must tweak it to the best of your ability until it's spot-on. Master projecting your melodies out to the world, because those are usually your hooks stuck in your head trying to manifest.

Also try to refrain from using profanity hooks and bars because the radio will have to do way more edits cutting and bleeping out a lot of your content. Plus the parent always buys clean rap version.

- Chapter 4 -

"Tempo" (Beats)

I'd like to start this chapter off paying homage to all the musical engineers and pioneers to pave the way before us. Along with our ancestral African roots, where the tribes first started with the beat of the drums by hand. Also the rhythmic dancing, chanting, jumping, and gyrating of the hips.

To the same drums and tempo we still use and move to this very day.

They were hip-hop before we knew what hip-hop was. They just used different names for it.

And that same tempo we vibe to is so effective and vibrant that non-African descendants are still moved and influenced by its spiral impact heavily.

Everything you learnt in the previous chapter have to be aligned with tempo of the beat. Also your tempo with your flow and hooks.

A tempo is the pace or rate of speed of music or passage.

Therefore, you have your own pace and also the pace of the beat. You have to prompt.

You don't want to be rapping over the beat or under the beat. You want to be on tempo with the beat and delivery. Remember, catch your melody. And if you cannot, maybe you should pass on that particular beat or song.

You can find beats that fit your sound and more your style that matches you, and it will be some beats you just can't vibe to or catch. You have to be able to recognize this, pass and move on. Else you'll waste your time and maybe even get discouraged. That's why it's very important to distinguish this early on.

You'll have a lot of hang-ups and tough obstacles first starting off getting the swing of things and a true feel for your newfound craft. Again, you have to practice and work at perfection if you want to be great.

The term "riding the beat" is just like riding a wave. You have to be spot-on. Not all artists master this in particular.

Pimp C was a master at riding the beat spot-on. He owned it along with Andre 3000 from Outkast.

Whereas, Jay-Z bounces so swell on the beat with his words with a spot-on tempo, too.

However, Eminem specialized in speeding up, then slowing down his tempo. All while still staying on tempo with the beat. He mastered manipulating his tempo to the beat, and clearly found his God-given talent. To be honest, I believe he is one of those artists that can spit to any beats you throw in front of him, which is very complex.

Let's start off with some basics. If you have more of a slower rap style or hyphenated, I would suggest you rap to a slower tempo beat. And if you have more of a rapid chopper rap style, I would suggest a faster upbeat tempo.

For example, you don't see Busta Rhymes album full of slow tempo beats. Instead they are fast uptempo beats to match and keep up with his tempo. And everyone vibes to Busta Rhymes tempo, especially at his live concerts. He is truly a prime example.

This applies to rappers with a more Southern Texas style where they like to rap to a slower, more chopped-n-screwed tempo beat. They obviously wouldn't sound right on a rapid Busta Rhymes type tempo beat.

Another example to look at is R&B, and an R&B artist don't sing to rap beats. Not because they can't. It's because they already know their pace, so they wouldn't dare sing to a Lil John crunk type tempo.

Also rappers do be featured on R&B tracks, but wouldn't dare to do their whole album at an R&B tempo unless you got talent like Drake, which is rare.

You must always be on tempo with your pace and the beat, spot what beats you can eat, versus the ones to delete.

In this process, some artists actually go thru a scroll of beats to find one of their liking or fits more of their tempo. Then begin writing or freestyling to begin their creative works.

Other artists prefer to write their complete song first and afterwards find a beat to match perfect, which is still a tasking and could be difficult if you don't master your self-tempo first.

One of the main reasons why is because you now have to adjust your lyrics and hook to fit the exact tempo of the beat. Else it won't be a match or a direct hit. People listen clear so they will definitely know you're off-key and your tempo and delivery is way off. Picture a city bus versus a motorcycle. They don't match up together. And that's how people will see it, if your tempo off and unprofessional.

Professionalism goes a long way no matter how hardcore of a rapper you are. Executives and people in the industry love working with people/artists that are professional and ethical and know what they are doing. They don't not want to babysit or hold your hand every step of the way. Nor do they have the time.

Have you ever heard an artist on the radio that you thought sucks, or you can do 10 times better and blow them out the water? Well, if so, that is because they are very professional and hard workers and mastered that. Along with being a people person. Followed by their strong drive. They are looked at as very ambiguous and ambitious. So people are more willing to take a chance with them on developing betterment at their craft, which in some cases works, and others don't. It's a toss-up but is highly possible.

YouTube is an amazing platform for free beats. Or simply Google free beats. This is only if you just starting off with no money or studio time and equipment. Plus this can help complete your song and hurry to get your timely music out.

Once you use these social outlets, you can put what type of artist beats you like or fits your style. Like you would search:

Example: Free beat search

Nipsey Hussle type beats

And the results will pop up. You can go thru them all to your liking. Another example is:

Example: Free beat search

21-Savage/Migos type beats

This will give you a concoction type sound of both artists you searched beats. It will be a similar sound as if the 2 artists did a collabo dope track.

Another option is you can just look up free beats of all the new up-and-coming hit beat makers and rip their beat and eat.

However, the flip side to this is some musical platforms and social media platforms won't let you upload your tracks because the beat is registered already to the beat maker/ producer. It may say you don't own the rights to the music even tho the beat maker put it online as free.

The beat makers do this to protect their work of art so nobody steals and takes credit for their hit beat produced. For the most part they want you to spit a hot 16 and a fire hook to blow up using their beat. This is because it will bring them more business and get their name and sound out there to the world and industry.

Then you have beat makers and producers like Dr. Dre, Swizz Beats, Mannie Fresh, and Timberland who can match damn near any artist's style and tempo Also, they charge 6 to 7 figures, but it's well worth a just about guaranteed hit. Actually these individuals' beats been known to make and carry the artist. Now that's powerful vibes and talent.

The beat is so important because it moves not just your song along, but the audience, too. Even little kids will bounce to a good beat and sometimes attempt to sing the hook.

So the beat is definitely the essence of hip-hop. It's just like watching a movie without the big screen. I mean you can hear it but not see what's going on. Therefore, it wouldn't have the same effect. And vice versa without the beat and tempo of hip-hop.

Stay on tempo and find your tempo and always master catching your beat. It's fun.

- Chapter 5 -

"Versatile"

Ty Dollar Sign can rap and sing. He sings his own hooks and spits his own 16s. This makes him versatile.

TI can go from his trap music style to a more nonchalant suit-and-tie style with R&B artists like Robin Thicke and Justin Timberlake. And usually when R&B artists reach out to you for a feature means you're versatile or simply a hot artist.

Dougie Fresh is a human beatbox machine. Just about any key, symbol, snare or beat he can do and more. Plus own unique special features he can do as well.

Of course it's a lot of people that can b-box, too, but not versatile like Dougie Fresh. Nowadays technology is growing so fast people don't b-box as much.

These three artists are all unique at their craft. This is three different ways I wanted to give you an example of versatility.

However, you can be versatile in many different ways and areas.

Versatile is turning with ease from one thing or position to another or having many aptitudes like Cardi B rapping English and Spanish.

Basically, can you switch your style up? Can you add a different element? Can you rap and produce beats? Can you rap fast and switch up your flow and tempo in the same 16 without going off beat?

You get the point. And just because you can rap and sing doesn't automatically make you versatile. Versatility is something you master as an M.C., too. So you have to work at it. First is discovery.

How can you discover your versatility, or if you're versatile at all? And remember not all of us are versatile. Whereas, some of us are naturally versatile.

You start this process off by exploring new options and trying new features. Add elements and see if it works or fits you.

You're discovering your hidden talents, too, by this process because you challenging yourself to go outside of your craft, which can be highly rewarding if you discover something groundbreaking that only you as an M.C. bringing to the table.

Innovation really helps you to not just create but discover something new inside of you. Remember you have to challenge yourself first.

This is why you see artists like Kanye West go to Paris and Wyoming. Not to found themselves because they already know and establish themselves. This process is a sole discovery from innovation. So they can hear themselves think, create, motivate, and get those creative wheels turning.

I seen one artist play live on a drum set and rap at the same time and on beat. Then he did a 16 in reverse. It was dope. He was definitely versatile. However, only he had to discover that talent of versatility thru trying. Going outside his element of just being a church drummer boy or just an M.C.

The challenge to yourself on versatility is

1. What am I good at?

2. What different element to try?

3. What do I like?

4. How can I innovate it?

The very first question is what am I good at for a reason. This is another trick of the trade. Because usually things you good at come natural to you. Once you perfect that, it makes you become great.

The key is to find the areas or things you excel in, then play with it, manipulate it, switch it up a few different ways. Work it out, and it will work out.

- Chapter 6 -

"Different Style"

Hip-hop is the genre of music which rap is classified under. So if you go into a music store, you will ask where is their hip-hop section, and it will say Hip-Hop/Rap.

It's different styles of rap even though hip-hop is its own genre of music alone.

You have gangster rap, which is more hardcore rap music. There is pop rap, which is popular music which people call commercial. Usually the stuff you hear streaming or on the radio.

There is underground rap, which is the exact opposite of pop rap. Some of these artists sold thousands or millions underground. Not all are local artists, and some have distribution or record deals, too.

Then there is all the different styles within the style or the M.C.s have created, validated, influenced, etc. Such as trap rap, chopped-n-screwed, thizzle rap, mumble rap, mainstream rap, local rap, harmony rap, animated rap, versatile rap, gutta rap, and so much more.

Every coast usually has its own sound. Every region and demographic has its own unique sound. Like East Coast rap, Southern, Midwest, West Coast, etc.

It's not one set style or way to rap. And this what makes rap music so versatile and universal. You can get anyone to vibe with you regardless of language barriers. Also, just because hip-hop started in New York, or New York is the U.S. birthplace, doesn't mean you have to rap with any East Coast style unless you prefer it or it's your style even if you live on the West Coast.

Old Dirty Bastard from Wu-Tang Clan was the best animated rapper. He owned it and was live. So whatever style you classify yourself under, own it and master it. In this chapter I had to make you aware and educate you on the different styles of rap.

- Chapter 7 -

"Freestyle"

Freestyle is the auxiliary to hip-hop. Freestyling is something every rap should do every day with or without a beat. Not only to sharpen your skills as an M.C., but because this develops mind, vocabulary, versatility, tempo, and style of formulating.

Freestyling is also very therapeutic. Helps you to vent yourself expressively. Also a stress reliever.

Freestyle means to come off the top of your head unrehearsed or unwritten. Just you and your creative thoughts matching your words consecutive to a rhyming melody.

This is mainly impulse and people say whatever they feel or comes to mind. However, you, too, can master this art form.

The same way you formulate the bars in your head as you write them.

With freestyling, you don't have to freestyle a 16 or a hook. Even though that would be dope and showcase your skills. It's just your utter word play.

When you freestyle and a bar don't rhyme, still keep going even if you mess up. This how you get better at it. And it's that same concept, think before you act.

If you can be a bar or two ahead of yourself, you'll know what you about to make rhyme next verse, scattering your brain for something quick that matches.

However, you don't want to sound premeditated. Then people will say you wrote that or you spitting some written stuff and not really freestyling, which some people do because they can't freestyle for nothing in the world, including known artists to this day.

This is considered cheating because it's all written. However, the artist don't just rob his/her fans, they rob themselves the most. Also the ability to create to push themselves further.

How do you freestyle is the question. With no pen or pad. First, you relax and clear your mind, meaning your nerves to settle down and project your verbs and nouns forward.

You pick a subject matter. For example, foreign cars. You try to rap about every foreign car you can think of from Bugatti to Maserati.

Keep your pace going. And remember, you have to catch the beat and ride it to your best ability. The same rules apply as if you rapping on your track except it's all freestyling.

All of us have freestyle in us, we just have to know how to trigger it to manifest correctly. You should keep practicing it until you grasp it and remember without no cheat sheets. All innovating and verbal word playing.

If you feel it in your head and you're in a public place, spit it out. Express yourself freely in a low tone, you don't have to make a scene. It's healthy for you and your career.

- Chapter 8 -

"Cipher"

Ciphers are the most illest in hip-hop. Cipher circles is fun to be in, also fun to watch. Because it showcases the M.C. true skills as an artist. Usually with multiple people watching, listening, and around.

Ciphers is like a freestyle convention. All M.C.s are freestyling. If you watch the hip-hop awards every year, you'll see at the beginning after commercial breaks new and known artists all spitting freestyle flows.

This is where you see lyrical word play, tongue twisters, versatility, and bars-on-bars. It's dope and bring us all back to the origin of hip-hop.

A cipher is a circle goes around usually freestyling or rapping. However, you can have or start a cipher anywhere you desire. At school, on a bus, train, basketball court, and one of my favorites, in the car. This is because music is always on, and usually we pump each other up and fuel off each other to spit freestyle of straight gas.

The old saying is true. If you want to be a lawyer, go to law school around other people practicing law for the bar exam.

If you want to rap, you should be around others that also rap. Then you call rappers up your age that's just starting or been doing it for awhile to start a cipher.

You guys can get a cipher going anywhere, remember, from basements, studios, to round tables. The sole purpose is to test and sharpen your skills. Plus the feedback you get from people is priceless because this gives you direction.

If someone says you sound like their favorite rapper, you may want to switch it up and find more your voice and sound that matches you. If someone says your rap is corny or sucks, maybe you should go back to the drawing board and practice harder.

It's a rough world. Everyone is entitled to their opinion. This helps you to get better and see the things you don't see. Take it as constructive criticism and better yourself for the next cipher.

- Chapter 9 -

"Ad Lib"

Ad libs are universal and also versatile, too. As you starting to see how truly hip-hop is really about creativity. You are performing your verbal canvas to the world.

Young Jeezy had that "Jeah" ad lib.

Desiigner have a "BBDDATT!" rapid gunfire ad lib that's just a sound.

DMX actually growls like a dog as an ad lib, which is highly unique and dope. Also fits him and his style and image.

Ad lib is to recite, spoken at one's pleasure, without limits, or to compose without practice. Usually this is a rapper's signature or trademark sound or saying.

There is some sharp and dope ad libs M.C.s create. It don't have to be one certain way or for your whole career. People get tired of the same old sound and saying and can grow sick of you as an artist, so be careful not to burn yourself or spotlight out before you can truly shine.

To this day, I think Master P's "Uughh" ad lib was the most influential because not just the world was saying it, but other M.C.s years to follow. It had that much of an impact.

How to create your own personalized ad libs is to ask yourself:

1. What is my rap name?

2. What's my imagery?

3. What's my theme?

4. How can I use elements synonyms to project my signature sound?

For instance, if you are named after a sword, you can make a "Ching!" sound of hitting or a "Swoosh" sound for slicing or chopping.

DJ Khaled is a D.J. promoter and producer. His theme is all promotional and advertises himself. Famous ad lib saying, "We the best!"

It's not hard to create ad libs, no wrong or right way. Just stay within the 4 ways I shared above as guideline. You don't want to contradict who and what you saying you are. Besides, it wouldn't match or sound right, because it won't fit in a verbal sense.

Your crowd is the biggest critics and will hold you accountable, especially if you're an established artist with a household name.

Look at it as a challenge to find your trademark saying and signature sounds.

Then your original ones you first create will change for the better. Some rappers utter anything that comes to mind.

The beauty again is it's all your creative space to create your imagery as you see fit to project. All fun and challenging your inner talent and innovation.

However, an ad lib is optional. You don't have to have one. Some rappers just simply say their names or don't use ad libs, period. Nothing beats a try. It may help you discover your mark.

- **Chapter 10** -

"Create Own Sound, Style, & Theme" (Innovation)

Now that you have learnt the basics, in this chapter I'll show you how to create and get your certified artistry.

To define innovation clearly is the introduction of something new. Ideas, method, or devices, and to make changes.

This will be your main tool in this process. Always innovate to formulate and you will come up with your own new content.

Stylize is to conform to a style, especially to represent or design according to a pattern or style rather than according to nature or tradition.

In developing your own style, first classify it. Starting off, you must figure out what style of artist you are. Of course not just your demographic. You can have a down South style from the East Coast and fit more into a trap music rap style.

However, you have to look what is in you. Maybe you are more suave, smooth style. Poetic, soulful, tongue twister, or even animated style.

The rap in the mirror trick is great to help in the area, too, because you can get a clear visual and audio. And you may discover you have a truly unique sound or a new style. And the world always love people with a distinctive sound where 50 years from now people will still automatic recognize your voice.

Imagery is important because you don't want to have a skate-or-die rap style and performing in a suit and tie. You would want to be in all skateboarding attire. You want to fit into your image you project.

Also you have to convey your message, movement, dance, image, theme all in one to fit your style of rap within your style. You don't want nothing to contrast against anything you project.

This discovery process will take some time, which is good because it means you working at it. Not one M.C. stays the same in one spot. They go thru growth and development process, too. Their first album is always followed up by a different style and growth for their sophomore album and so on.

Please don't force it or you will miss your niche attempting to rush to sound like everyone else streaming. Trust me, it will come. Everyone can respect any artist at a developmental stage.

Theme is a subject or topic of artistic representation. Also a melodic subject of a musical composition or movement.

Two prime examples of a theme is the Naked Cowboy playing the guitar and singing in his underwear in New York City, Times Square. Yes, he sings and is a guitarist, but his theme is Naked Cowboy. He fits his style with imagery from the cowboy hat and being naked and made a name for himself. Some people come to New York just to see him and take pictures with him.

The second example is WWF. The wrestler called The Undertaker had his own grave scary theme music. His music, image, and persona all were very intimidating to his wrestling opponent. This was his come-out music and it would play until he walked slowly with a stern face into the ring.

Your persona is the personality that a person projects in public. You can use all the same type elements as a checklist to create your theme.

1. Subject or topic

2. Representation

3. Music to composition or movement

You can even have a theme move or dance if you so please, long as you create whatever you desire that fits your style and image.

Sound is the last part to your creative process, and I saved the best for last because sound is so important. It's everything literally is this newfound verbal medium crafting of yours.

Sound is sensational of hearing, stimulus to hearing, and convey a certain impression.

Your sound is your whole persona of how people will look and listen to see if you fit the part. Therefore, match it to your sleek image.

You can play with your sound. Try a lot of different styles. Go outside of your comfort zone and challenge yourself. You may have mixture of styles and versatile. Come up with your own concoction of style. And those are dope, too That's where you hear an artist but can't quite point the finger on his style. They may sound a bit like Kendrick Lamar/Travis Scott or a little like Drake/Future sound. However, it's their concoction sound and they own it.

You can choose to take this mixed style approach, but sound like the two of your own unique sounds. Your better and best sound all in one. Not biting someone's work of art, which is technically called infringement.

You want to be ingenious in all of this creating own self-image and exclusive sound. Ingenious is being marked by special aptitude at discovering, inventing or contriving. Originality, resourcefulness, and cleverness in conception or execution.

Therefore, ingenuity is a key element to spring a style into life.

Now you have work to do. It's not soul searching, so don't overwhelm or stress yourself. It's development of your beginning, middle, and end.

This is your signature mark, sound, and style. Also inception to your building process. The saying is true, nothing was built overnight and last. Those pyramids in Egypt weren't built in a day or even one year. However, 5,000 years later, they still stand, still in alignment.

Which is the same timeless music you can create with an everlasting prominent impact. Years from now your kids' kids can still vibe to your sounds. You must believe in yourself and hold steadfast at your craft.

- Chapter 11 -

"Create Own Label" (Independent)

Now that you are in the swing of things and created your own signature style and sound, you may want to choose to be your own boss and go a more independent route by creating your own record label. Similar to a D.I.Y. (do-it-yourself) approach.

Which isn't a bad thing long as you aware of the dos and don'ts and ups and downs. It's always risk but there is also reward, too.

Some artists have a more entrepreneur spirit and drive while others don't like being told by a boss what, when, or how to do their music and want to retain their exclusive rights and revenue to their own creative works of art produced.

Just about every older record label or superstar story movie shows artists getting ripped off clean from blocked contracts to producers, road managers, assistants—you name it. All from them being new to the industry and not educating themselves.

This is optional. All artists don't have to go an independent route. It's a lot and can take away from your music time producing and perfecting, especially if you have additional artists on your label. You will have a full plate and need to hire staff for all aspects and a lot of paperwork to oversee and process.

However, it's all possible. First, you want to register your own label after you created the name and logo.

You start off by searching the name you choose in the USPTO (United States Patent and Trademark Office) online to see if it's available or taken. And they will also give you a guideline about certain abbreviations and numbers with names. Also what is and isn't acceptable as a logo. You can also print it out from their site.

The next step is registry with BMI online or ASCAP. You can use either one or both. This is for your royalties. Your earnings every time your song is played. Also to register your record label as a company.

It will be fees and applications to fill out, too. I prefer ASCAP. However, BMI has its perks, too, and not as complex online and gives you different options. Go to BMI.com/Register/Application and Fees.

ASCAP is American Society of Composers, Authors and Publishers. They have a New York and California location if you choose to write them for any general information.

Once you go online www.ascap.com/about/howjoin.asp it will tell you if you're eligible. It will be two applications. A publisher application, which includes membership agreement, processing fee form, and TIN (taxpayer identification number) and certificate, a W-9 form.

The second application is a writer application, which membership agreement, processing fee form, and W-9 form, too.

You'll need to do both applications to establish your exclusive rights and registry.

If you are an LLC (limited liability co.), don't forget to put that. To get your incorporation (Inc.) or LLC, check your local state listings Revenue Departments.

You can get your EIN (employer identification number) thru IRS.gov. Then set you up a business account for your label.

Remember to read everything before submitting and paying. You must educate yourself. I'm not a lawyer, I am just showing you how to register your own label and your exclusive rights.

Go to www.uspto.gov to read over all the briefs and facts along with all the trademark and unfair competition laws.

Some brand names, trade names, slogans, and phrases may be entitled to protection under those laws relating to unfair competition, while others may be entitled under state or federal trademark laws. So please, it's a must to educate yourself and don't be so eager to rush and just complete the applications and pay the fees. You will be left scratching your head clueless if your app gets declined or rejected.

You must register your label with United States Patent & Trademark Office or go online www.uspto.gov.

It will be Federal Trademark Statute covers trademarks and service marks, certain application forms, and other related materials are available, too.

Once you have successfully created and started your independent label, you want to get a decent distribution deal or a distributor for your supply and demand of records and sales.

Next your job is to do a talent search for hot new unique artists to represent your new label accordingly. Then you can compete with the big dogs. Your long-term goal is to get IPO (initial public offering) stocks of record company.

- Chapter 12 -

"Register Rap Name & Logo" (Trademark)

This is very important and can be very costly in the end. So I'd highly suggest you trademark and register your name, logo, or animate face or theme. Your exclusive right you are entitled to.

Regardless if you choosing to go more of the independent route or searching for a sponsor and major record deal, everyone must register their rap name or pseudonym (fictitious name), stage name, and professional name for the following reasons of protecting.

My first example is a foreclosure. Yes, a foreclosure on terminating a home mortgage and then taking possession of the mortgaged property, leaving the bank that you used to finance the property to sell for the remaining debt not equity.

Well, this leaves someone to buy the property you had equity and half paid off for below the asking price at a steal versus all the money you put into it and your original listed price per comps in the neighborhood value per home. It works same way in music industry, someone can steal your hard-earned works and rights.

Another example is a foreclosure on a patent for an inventor. If you don't pay your patent when timeframe expires, it leaves it open to the public and patent sharks who get rich off of people that didn't update their patent or simply look for old patents of people that passed away or the device is too old but still may generate little royalties.

Just simple as these listed examples are musical sharks trolling to make a quick buck from your misguided or uneducated first-timer rookie mistakes.

I won't expose no artists' names because it's their personal business. I've seen artists pay millions to get or buy their own rap names back after they blow up to superstar status from not owning the exclusive rights to their names.

I'm sharing this with you to educate you and save you the money and headache legal and lawyer fees all in one.

However, the good news is to avoid this common error, simply go to register your name or names and logos, etc.

The United States Patent and Trademark Office (www.uspto.gov) Commissioner for Trademarks and Trademark Assistance Center@uspto.gov will have all the info on laws and protections you're entitled to. Federal and state trademarks. Also the unfair competition laws like mentioned in last chapter is mandatory.

Remember words, phrases, symbols, or designs that distinguish the goods or services from one party to another is all under USPTO. Some brand names, slogans, trade names, phrases may all be entitled to protection under laws.

Again, educate yourself and you will be fine and do great because all of your loose ends will be tied. Plus you will be all legit and ready to shock the world with a successful career. And make sure to register your rap name with ASCAP and do a writer's application www.ASCAP.com/writersapplication.

- Chapter 13 -

"Social Media Platforms" (PR)

Your musical debut. This is your choice to decide if you going to do a mixtape, single, EP album. Whatever one you think you want to start off with first. This will be your project.

I would do a single or a mixtape to start before your album. Your sole purpose is to create a buzz and get your music out there and heard.

Obviously starting off you are an unknown artist. So it's your duty to make yourself known and establishing yourself as a household name and possibly brand, too.

What better way to get your music out and heard than many of the various social media platforms? Especially because it's not expensive, infinite, and reaches millions to the world wide web.

If you're hot and dope artist, you shouldn't have a problem being seen or heard unless you're projecting yourself to limited platforms.

Of course it's YouTube number 1. However, you have WorldStar and a lot of different social platforms for videos. Or you can start your own channel and have all your latest music and videos on YouTube for viewers and fans to subscribe to.

If you don't have a video budget or no means, you can use different mobile video apps like OneShot, Triller, and Flipagram.

Also it's other mobile apps available at Google Play Store for mixing and producing your music, too. Like BandLab and SoundCloud. Just about anything you can think about from voice recorders, beat machines, autotunes, etc., is all available at Play Store.

Social musical platforms such as Apple Music, Spotify, iTunes, and Tidal are all places where you can upload your music and get it available on all possible outlets to be heard.

Which process thanks to technology is way easier than the hustle and shuffle game 25 years ago where M.C.s would stand out in the freezing cold just at a chance of catching Daymond Dash to hand him their mixtape or try to spit a 16 for him.

Puffy Combs had M.C.s running to buy him a cheesecake while others would go to Universal with CDs attempting to get it to an AR to hear. It was like a battle of the bands and took hard drive an artist had to pull stunts.

Tupac Shakur had to carry crates for Humpty Hump and went on tour with digital underground just to get on and heard.

Whereas, Biggie Smalls had more of a battle rap buzz taking out M.C.s all over Brooklyn to get the streets' attention and eventually Puffy Daddy. More of a word-of-mouth approach and hustling.

I'm pretty sure we wouldn't hear from half the artists now if it wasn't for social media platforms. Some artists released a mixtape and blew up without no deals or from one hot single on social media. Chance the Rapper did it all from musical platforms solo and all the way to the mainstream radio without no deals either. Anything is possible with your drive and ambition. Most of all, work ethic. Keep putting out all your works of art to be heard around the clock.

You can use any method, outlets, formulas to get your music out and heard. The goal is radio spins, and you get them automatic if people are streaming your music from the data, videos, and playback. It helps you get to the Top 100 Billboard Charts, and if you make it to the Top 20, great job. However, the Top 10 you really are well on your way to being a superstar and world knowing your name.

At this point you want your music to stay consistent. Don't get caught up in the hype and stuck in awe on yourself. You don't want to be a one-hit wonder. It downplays your talent and hard grind it took you to writing and creating or performing your work of art.

One day they love you, the next day they love someone else. So stay persistent, relevant, and evolve with the times and all your designs.

Some artists are known for using publicity stunts to get on and don't believe in PR (public relations) or a such thing as bad publicity. They simple believe good or bad publicity is still publicity, long as they a trending topic, and usually see them all over social media doing some bizarre things for a buzz and attention. It's just some artists' motto.

Publicity is information with news value issued to gain public attention or support and acclaim.

Public relations or PR is the business of fostering public goodwill toward a person, firm, or institution.

A prime example of goodwill and PR is Chance the Rapper donating a million dollars to Chicago Public School.

This good PR is the type of public image you want to have because it helps you not just to be likable, but gains more fans, viewers, and followers, which equal more record sales and radio spins.

Basically your name should be tied to all righteous endeavors. All artists have a responsibility and duty that comes with having a voice because it influences your fanbase and audience.

Anything you do, people follow. Just like being a trendsetter or being a brand. Any new thing, style, or saying they will use, become, or do.

Social media outlets are fun because you can use many different tactics and avenues to promote. Once it catches, it will spread like wildfire because how social media works. People share with their family, friends, co-workers, etc., always asking if they heard this new song or seen this video. And word of the mouth, plus people's curiosity to see whatever everyone sees and buzzing about and click on yours.

- Chapter 14 -

"Marketing"

Marketing plan for your music and brand such as shirts, shoes, drinks, or hats. Whatever you choose to brand with your name and music as a product of your works and sound or image.

If you in the industry of hip-hop, marketing is very important and highly rewarding. Everyone has different marketing plans or tactics.

Of course the underlying issue in marketing is profit. Along with supply and demand deal in. Also vending, retail, wholesale. It's consumer based.

In the art of buying and selling, you need to know your price per unit, ROI (return on investment), and sale sheets.

Typical record stores buy CDs and merchandise based on the artist sales and inventory space. Usually they buy in bulk at a cheaper or wholesale rate per unit.

They buy from the record label or distributor. The artist is usually paid off by them. Afterward the music store is left to sell your music. If your album sales isn't flying off the shelf, then they most likely won't fill another 5,000-unit order. If you're sure of your product and merchandise, you should not have no problem in this department.

However, if you're not signed and want to sell your CD at a knowing record store, too, you ask the manager.

Once you speak with the manager, you ask him/her about their policy for local artists or private vendors. Some will let you set up a small stand in-store and will charge you a percentage per unit you sell in their store.

For example, if you selling your CD $8.00, they will keep $5.00 for hosting and selling. So you keep $3.00 or whatever their percentage is.

This is an older concept but still marketing. Today a lot of music stores are mostly going out of business because of online sales and you can simply just download or get free music as you please.

Tell yourself how are you going to profit and make yourself a known brand at the same time with all this free music streaming all over the place.

I first off would do an all-in-one website for your music, brand, and all merch. You can have links or hyperlinks to them also.

Some artists even share their music for free and rely on their brand and merch sales. I would only recommend this if you have a well-established brand, not for starters.

You may just want to simply upload your registered music on musical platforms to sell and market for your best interest for starters or if you can't find a suitable marketing plan.

To this day I think Chance the Rapper, DJ Khaled, Puffy, Jay-Z, Nipsey Hussle all master marketing. If you pay attention to their different and innovative angles, it's dope.

To create your marketing plan, you must ask yourself your game plan:

1. What am I marketing?

2. What is my structure and volume?

3. What is my goal?

4. How can I make it better?

5. Is there any innovation angles?

6. What can I do for further promo?

7. Price and profit and ratio?

8. Can I market off PR?

9. Out with old, in with new method?

10. What is product feedback rate?

Promo is short for promotion, like some artists give stores, radio stations, fans promo CDs, shirts, posters, etc., for promotional standard, which is part of smart marketing, too. The more people to hear, the more people to share. The more people to share, the more people to buy. And remember you getting your music out to be heard and build your audience along with establishing your household name. Online it's plenty of marketing plans or books available for you to further educate.

- Chapter 15 -

"Ghost Writer"

A ghost writer is to write for and in the name of another person.

Usually ghost writers sign a non-disclosure agreement form where they cannot disclose the person or artist they writing for that they used a ghost writer or it's actually the ghost writer work of creative arts, instead of artist performing hit song and exclusive lyrics.

Ghost writers usually get paid in huge amounts and can be other M.C.s for other M.C.s that may not have dope bars or so creative.

My favorite ghost writer line is from Jay-Z. He says:

"Ghost writer, for the right price I'll make ya ish tighter."

Even though a lot of behind-the-scenes ghost writers are used and responsible for huge hit songs selling millions for the artist, it is frowned upon in the hip-hop community and industry. Even though it's all business, it's not all you. It's someone else's skillset and sound. So it's looked at as the M.C. don't have real skills and needs a cheat sheet, which people can perceive you as a straight out gimmick with just a people's image. And those don't last too long once exposed. It can be like career suicide.

It's okay to ghost write for others, but you shouldn't have no one ghost write for you because it can backfire and it shows lack of skills on a new artist. Like you got discovered or signed by a fluke.

Some people choose to have a ghost writer though. It's whatever fits you and your rights. It's all part of hip-hop, so I had to share with you what a ghost writer is and does.

For all the M.C.s with dope creative lyrics that's versatile, I'd highly recommend being a ghost writer for other artists in need. It's a lucrative payoff.

You don't have to be a signed artist to ghost write or even a known artist. You can simply fill an inquiry of public or classified ad someone post, which you can find online, too.

They range from ghost writers from R&B, rap, all genres of music and scripts from films to books. Basically like a freelance writer does. You can take on any job that hires you in that field based on your skills.

I would suggest you refer to any body of works you did. All your hottest projects or any new feature you add to the table.

Create a résumé and have it handy to email the inquirer to see and showcase your skills along with your audio. Don't forget to list all your versatility.

You may just stumble upon a new side hustle or possibly career as a ghost writer.

- Chapter 16 -

"Sampling vs. Remixing"

Sampling is using piece or various from prior sound or records.

An example of sampling is what Drake did on his "Nice for What" track where he sampled Lauryn Hill's '90s hit song, which came out dope.

Sampling is allowed and very much hip-hop, too. They usually make hit concoctions. Puffy Daddy made a lot of hits sampling, too. A lot of older artists and R&B artists used a lot of samples in the '80s and '90s especially.

However, you don't want to sample something and do a horrible job on representation and sampling.

You must also get permission of the exclusive rights to the music or what you sampling. Even if the artist is deceased, you would still reach out to their parties, entities, estates.

In samples, you can use pieces or one piece. Just make sure it don't sound like you stole the old hit song vs. sampling it.

It has been artist or more than one artist to sample the same songs. And all of this is doable in hip-hop. Just try to top the other artist before your version.

Remixing is to make a new or different form of. This was another thing Diddy was good at producing remixes. Missy Elliott had some dope remixes, too.

Again, this is an element allowed and part of hip-hop, too, which you need to still get permission to the person that retains exclusive rights to the music before you remix their song.

Remixes is fun and dope if done right and the correct artist. Have you ever heard corny remix on the radio, like wow, they messed up a perfectly put-together hit song?

Nowadays you see more and more artists remixing their own hit songs with more featured artists or in Spanish.

You can remix just about any song. Whereas, sampling piece don't always work or fit within your signature style. Or simply not timely and people not responding how you would like. It's a gamble and a flip side.

However, it's a science behind everything if you know to formulate your style with any music pattern, musical staff, or 4-part singing chorus. Adaptability is essential in remixing and sampling. Especially if you have an eye or ear for it.

I wouldn't suggest you do your whole album with all samples or remixes because it does cut away from your original content aspects. Just word of advice.

Hip-hop is what you make it and create.

- Chapter 17 -

"Branding Yourself"

When hip-hop first started, you didn't see artists branding themselves. Hip-hop has evolved with the "artistpreneur" concept, where they brand themselves along with their products and merchandise. From sneakers to alcohol, clothing lines, headphones, speaker bass box tubes, you name it, which is perpetual.

You can start branding yourself now before you establish your household name and get validation from the industry.

Create your products and follow your style. Don't go outside your lines of artistry works like explained in previous chapters.

Think about it this way. Say if you created a dope sneaker line and had a back-story behind it that people will love. You have 10 sneakers already finished products. Soon as you become a known artist, those 10 prototypes will become a reality and fly off the shelves.

It's property preparation and staying ahead and busy. Also puts your entrepreneur skills to the test.

You can brand anything you create. Put your signature brand name behind it, which works like you as an artist are endorsing the brand. It's like validating your own work with rubber stamp of approval, and the followers and fans is sure to follow suit.

Your back-story is important and acts as your logic behind your product and brand.

Graffiti is part of hip-hop, too. We don't see it so much in the older form. Nowadays artists evolved to tattoos, which is now part of hip-hop now, too. However, I would not recommend tatting your face just in case you don't become that established superstar. Reality is you will have to work in the workplace. Even being an entrepreneur and jumping into a suit and tie could hurt your sale volumes because presentation is everything. Unless you a multi-millionaire like Birdman, then who cares? I'm not against it, I just want you using your head to think first. Even though all the new M.C.s are doing it and it's part of them branding themselves creatively.

A brand is a class of goods identified as the product of a particular producer, firm, or individual.

Your checklist:

1. Create your brand.

2. What are you branding?

3. How are you branding it?

4. Your product and brand name should coexist.

5. Marketing and wide distribution.

You may find that you have a network of branding, and you have to kickstart your own projects at first until your brands are generating income. Of course once it's lucrative, people then want to jump aboard which investors, sponsors, and endorsement is all welcome and can be a great thing. It's your choice.

- Chapter 18 -

"Exhaust All Options"

Exhaust all your options. Not just limited to an M.C., you may be a better songwriter than a rapper. Or a producer, beat maker, video director, etc., it's all hip-hop. Don't just settle for rap alone.

Really we would have way more people in different areas of the hip-hop field if everyone wasn't just focused on the main rapping-part superstar. Not everyone is going to make it even with lyrical and dope skillset. Plus with the daily fierce competition out there.

I don't want you to get discouraged. I want you to also discover other things you excel in, too. It's a lot of producers and beat makers that started out rapping and to this day making more revenue than some actual artists.

You can use all these same creative elements and innovation methods and apply them into any aspect of hip-hop. The field is vast.

Some people are natural gifted. Have you ever seen a person play a keyboard that's dope and self-taught? He/She has automatic ear and feel for it. Each key they stroke is like they had been doing it for their whole lives.

Usually they all started off as hobbies before they realized their skillset people are in high demand for. Then they establish their name and brand themselves in the same way an M.C. does. Also the same drive and ambition.

Don't be afraid to try new things, irregardless how awkward it may feel at first.

Also music entities will hire you for your skilled services and expertise. Anywhere from ARs, executive officers, managers. Who knows? You can even be a hip-hop publicist or analyst. All relative to hip-hop and actual careers.

The saying is true: If you believe, you can achieve. First you have to conceive the notion, then manifest its existence.

Outro

The youth is the truth. I pray for you to find your way and innovate your creative style. I am an advocate for the youth and truly believe in you all and love you all for generations to come.

This book was meant to not just show you how to rap and the elementary teachings of hip-hop, but to enlighten you, motivate you, inspire you to bring out the best of you.

All people are created equal is true. However, all people don't share equal gifts and talent.

What we do have equal is the faculty of hearing along with the universal sound of music, melody, and rhythm.

Each person has their own unique sound, melody, and vibe.

A bird chirp may be nerve-racking. And a cricket chirp may drive you nuts, too. However, there is a melody and tune if you listen closely. The same with the raging winds, if you listen. And that is exactly what this book is set out to show you how to do. Tune into your inner self and melody. If you master this, you will peak at your craft and bring all your gifts and sounds to the world.

You don't need to be like nobody else. Be the best version of self. Because no one can't match your unique individuality. Maybe sound like, but not you—the truth.

Originality and versatility are key. Creativity equals longevity.

I wish you all success in the hip-hop industry. I thank you for taking the time out to educate yourself and reading the basics.

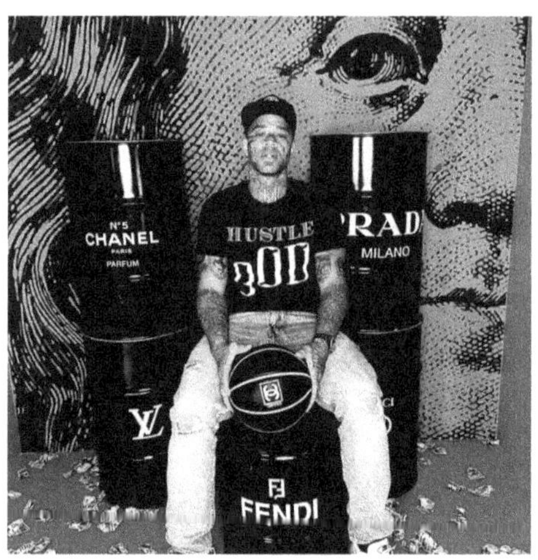

About Author

Hitachi Choparazzi is a New York City native, by the way of Omaha, who is currently incarcerated in level 5 solitary confinement in Florence, SMU-Eyman Complex, serving an illegal sentence awaiting on Supreme Court Appeal to correct his sentence with time served. The error forces him to serve 2 years extra.

He is an entrepreneur, tattoo artist turned author. Also the sole owner of Chop-a-Style Publishing and Productions, and the owner of Chatmon Sr. Literary Agency. He has written over 20 books and including scripts to pitch to Netflix. All this while he was incarcerated to start his reform act.

Founder and CEO of Billion-Dollar Blueprint and the BDB movement/youth movement, an innovator entrepreneurship where he believes everyone has their own blueprint, like everyone has their own unique thumbprint. Based on 3 core principles—Education, Elevation, and Innovation—which he teaches the youth and people how to format and discovery key. BillionDollarBlueprintmerch.com

The face of lockdown society movement along with the voice of lockdown society movement. IncarceratedLivesMovement. com #ILM #BDB

"I do this for y'all. I love y'all, rep y'all, and believe in y'all! I won't stop giving y'all all the raw stories as God bless them in my head. I have a hundred of them up there. Anybody that has a hot hand, send me samples or any comments, suggestions to my FB, IG Hitachi Choparazzi or email: orders@ chopastylepublishingllc.com Chop-A-Style Publishing LLC and Productions. TeflonLuv!"

Hitachi Choparazzi prides himself on having his own signature Chop-a-Style where he freestyles all his books. They all rhyme with innovation and original storylines. He writes prequels, sequels, trilogies, and more. Does it for the people who love to read and for all those incarcerated in state, federal B.O.P., county, and women's facilities. FB,IG,Tiktok, Twitter, YouTube-Hitachi Choparazzi

Emails: Hitachichoparazziauthor@gmail.com Billiondollarblueprintmerch.com

Chop-A-Style Publishing and Productions LLC

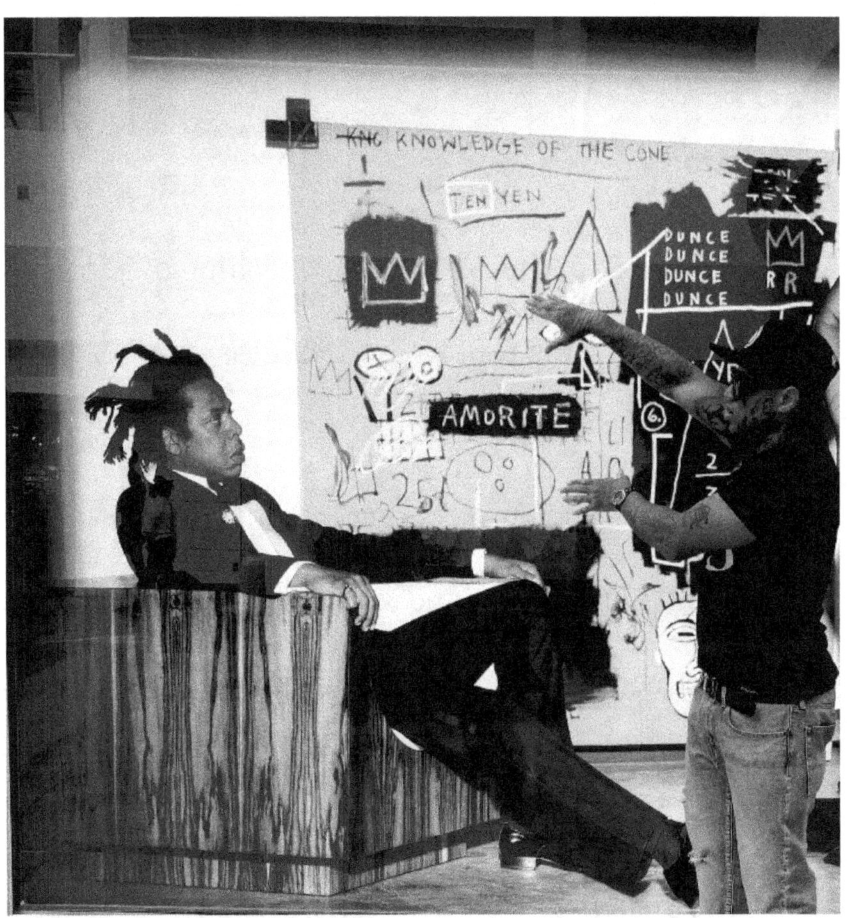

Hitachi Choparazzi pitching Billion Dollar Blueprint to Jay-z @ Scottsdale Fashion Square Mall AZ

Other Books and Scripts by the Author

Non-Fiction

- How to Rap; The Elementary Teaching of Hip-Hop

- How To Tattoo & Start-Up Business

- How To Digital Detox

- How To Start-Up a Food Truck Business

- How To Stop School and Mass Shootings: Dear Parents

- Incarcerated Lives Matter: The Hitachi Choparazzi Blueprint

- How to Love

- The Switch: A Social Awareness Self-Help

- Nipsey Hussle Lockdown Society Dedication–Tribute

- If Trayvon Martin Could Talk; Injustice

Fiction

- The Eagle and Weasel (1-5 series kids' book)

- She Go! (urban novel)

- Reality Show 3D-HD (urban novel)

- Hot Thots (urban novel)

- Liqz (urban novel)

- Paranormal Whisper (horror novel)

- Pimp of Da Ratchets (urban novel)

- Pimp of Da Ratchets II Vegas (urban novel)

- Pimp of Da Ratchets 3 Orange is Da New Pimp (urban novel)

- Hitachi (urban novel)

- Penitentiary Pimp (urban novel)

- Weasel Society (urban novel)

- The Big Pep and Plucker Story-She Go! Prequel (urban novel)

Screenplays/Scripts

- Top Notch

- Hot Thots

- Pimp of Da Ratchets

- Weasel Society

- Million Dollar Games–A Secret Society

- The Eagle and Weasel (animation)

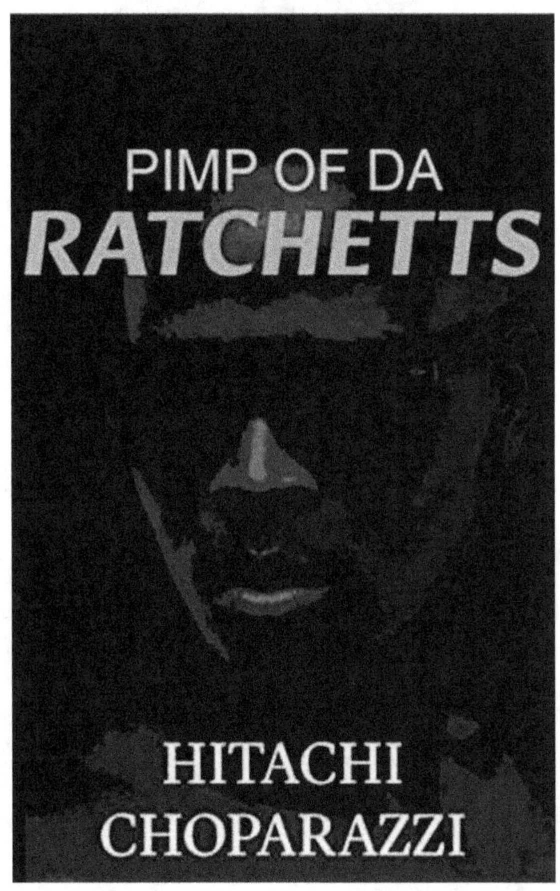

Available at Barnes and Noble and Amazon

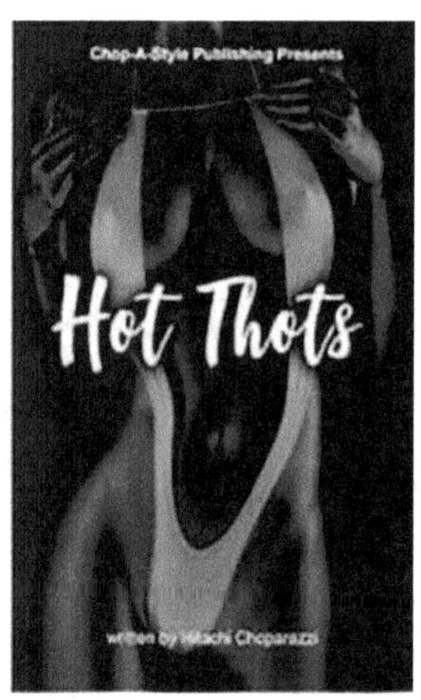

Welcome to the exclusive lives of 4 extremely hot THOTs. This book will show you how to spot a THOT. From THOT tops to THOT flops, all the way to THOT Snaps and claps.

This book is the first-ever with a double twisted love triangle. Watch as Chicago, LA, ATL, and Seattle THOTs entwine at Coachella.

Some on fleek and some looking cheap, but they all cheat! They all commit aTHOTery with their THOTery acts, shameless.

Raunchy, with steaming hot sex scenes to sex swings. From wild threesome ménages, and twerking, to bare-it-all raw. Too hot! THOT gum pop...

This page-turner is an eye-opener to the very end, with a bombshell-dropping, shocking ending. The secret life of THOTs

Available at Barnes and Noble and Amazon

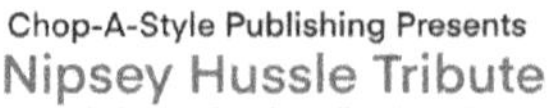

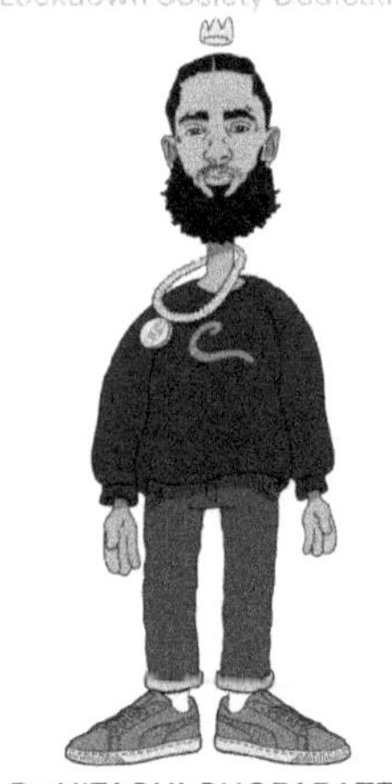

A lockdown society dedication and tribute to the late Nipsey Hussle the Great. To reflect the life of Nipsey Hussle, works, music, and art form. From him being prolific, visionary, influencer, community activist, humanitarian, revolutionary, philanthropist, radical entrepreneur, youth funding developer, and a reintegrating advocate, along with so much more of his innovation businesses and movements. The Marathon history and continuance. Nipsey's legacy, principles, and elements, along with his epic All Money In slogan and concept behind the brand.

This lockdown society tribute to Nipsey also is from the inside of an incarcerated author, Hitachi Choparazzi, that reflects the influence, inspiration, and motivation that Nipsey Hussle's music, message, and movements played a huge hand in people incarcerated transformation process and self-reforming, using time for them versus against them. Lockdown society didn't have a voice to show Nip love and give regards, respects, and gratitude for the seeing and believing he delivered to the inside. Most of all, to pay homage to a luv1 and a creator.

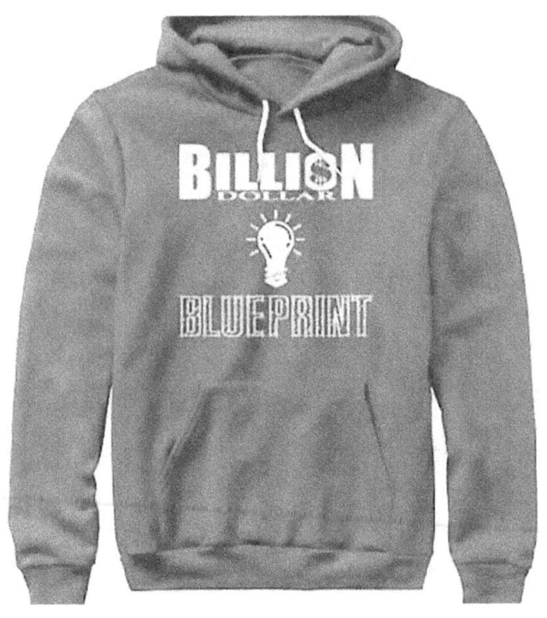

Billion Dollar Blueprint is a movement we challenge and inspire you to find your individual blueprint. Our mantra is "We believe everyone has their own blueprint like everyone has their own thumbprint". With these three core principles

Education

Elevation

Innovation

Hitachi Choparazzi is the founder and CEO. Orders available to support incarcerated businesses.

Orders available at: billiondollarblueprintmerch.com